ASK AESOP
Ancient Wisdom for Modern Dilemmas
DANIEL C. BRYAN

Ask Aesop, the first thematically indexed collection of 125 Aesop's fables, places his wit and wisdom at your fingertips.

Compiled with adolescents and adults in mind, the unique Thematic Keyword Index enables you to rapidly locate guidance on a broad range of issues, dilemmas, and human foibles, making it both a self-help book and an educational resource.

As a self-help book, it encourages you to gain new perspectives, to think around your problems, and to arrive at your own decisions. As an educational resource, *Ask Aesop* provides a springboard for pragmatic, secular discussions of morality.

Whilst the fables can be enjoyed for their own sake, *Ask Aesop* also provides ammunition for debates, barbed parting shots, and gems for after-dinner speeches.

After studying philosophy at the universities of Sussex and Cambridge, Daniel C. Bryan worked in education as a teacher, librarian, and careers co-ordinator.

PSYCHOLOGY / PHILOSOPHY / SELF-HELP / FABLES

ASK AESOP

ANCIENT WISDOM FOR MODERN DILEMMAS

125 FABLES WITH A UNIQUE THEMATIC KEYWORD INDEX

Daniel C. Bryan

Stick House Books

First published 2024
by Stick House Books
stickhousebooks@yahoo.com

Copyright © 2024 Daniel C. Bryan

The right of Daniel C. Bryan to be identified as the author of this work has been asserted by him in accordance with the Copyright, Designs and Patents Act 1988.

Typeset in Minion 12/16pt

Typesetting and book design by Keith Seddon, incorporating the author's modified medallion based on an image of Aesop found on a kylix dating from *c.* 470 BCE (Gregorian Etruscan Museum, Vatican City)

ISBN 978–1–304–93340–9

For my mother

Erika

&

In memory of my father

John

DARE TO BE WISE

Horace (65-8 BCE)
Epistles, Book 1, Epistle 2, ll. 39-40

CONTENTS

Preface	11
How to Use this Book	13
Who was Aesop?	15
Thematic Keyword Index	19
Aesop's Fables	55
Index of Fable Titles	183
Reader's Personal Notes	189

PREFACE

This book enables you to access rapidly Aesop's wise counsel on a wide range of issues.

The substantial number of books of Aesop's fables in print, ranging from illustrated children's books to academic collections, is a testament to his enduring popularity, yet none gives easy access to specific guidance. My frustration at the effort required to locate the right fable for a given topic or dilemma led me to retell a representative 125 fables, based on literal translations, and to devise a Thematic Keyword Index.

The Thematic Keyword Index identifies a fable that speaks to the dilemma you are facing, allowing you to see whether it sheds any light on your situation. To date, this is the only collection structured to make this possible.

In most cases, we should not expect a definitive answer. By engaging with fable, we open ourselves to new perspectives and the possibility of our everyday self

PREFACE

accessing the wisdom of our higher self. It's not a matter of being told what to think. A negative reaction to a moral or principle is at least as valuable to us as a positive reaction. Our response to the fable tells us where we stand. As free autonomous individuals, we remain responsible for our decisions and actions. Asking Aesop can aid us on this journey, but our decisions are our own.

If Aesop can't help us from across the void of over two-and-a-half millennia, then we might have a new kind of problem that wasn't around back then. It's unlikely, though, as it's all about our foibles and the principles and issues involved in co-existing with others.

That a compilation of this size cannot cover every desired line of enquiry, may disappoint at times. However, the practice of applying fables to everyday dilemmas can change how we position ourselves in the world – meeting difficulties with measured responses instead of instant reactions. Whilst my progress has been more aspirational than impressive, I hope you will join me on this road.

Above all, irrespective of whether the journey is uncomfortable or pleasant, Dare to be wise!

DANIEL C. BRYAN
Stroud, Gloucestershire, England
December 2023

HOW TO USE THIS BOOK

Aesop's fables can, of course, be enjoyed and learnt from in any order. However, if you have a specific problem, or are curious to know how Aesop's thought can be applied to a certain theme, turn to the **Thematic Keyword Index,** on page 19.

Keywords are followed by short phrases or sentences that indicate the insight, universal truth, or moral of the fable listed. If you cannot find the Keyword(s) you had in mind, try others with similar meanings. For example, 'TOUGH LUCK' is not listed, but 'BAD LUCK' and 'MISFORTUNE' are. The numbers in the Thematic Keyword Index refer to the number assigned to each fable in this collection.

If you are looking for a particular fable, turn to the **Index of Fable Titles** at the back of the book.

Remember, Aesop's fables express *principles* and *morals*. Ask yourself whether these apply to your situation.

HOW TO USE THIS BOOK

In most cases, the *events* and *characters* will not reflect your situation at all, unless you happen to be a lion or have a pre-Christian lifestyle. Furthermore, you may not agree with Aesop's point of view or the moral principle he is promoting. That does not matter: the aim is to *think around* your problem, to discover what *you* think. Sometimes that can only be found by first considering the views of others before embracing or rejecting them. Asking yourself why you agree or disagree may help you to untangle the principles and emotions of your dilemma.

Additionally, in keeping with the fables' original purpose, the **Thematic Keyword Index** allows you to locate appropriate fables for debates, educational purposes, and wedding-and-after-dinner speeches - in short, a valuable resource to have at hand.

WHO WAS AESOP?

Aesop is thought to have lived over two-and-a-half millennia ago, approximately between 620 BCE and 564 BCE. However, while his name is synonymous with many well-known fables, little can be said about his life with certainty.

Legend has it that he was born in either Cotiaeum, in Phrygia, or Sardis on the Greek island of Samos. At some point, he was enslaved and became the property of Iadmon, a citizen of Samos. It is said that his owner was so impressed with his use of fables to win arguments and settle disputes, that he gave him his freedom. This rebuffs the erroneous, common assumption that Aesop's fables were created *for* children (though, of course, they enjoy and greatly benefit from them).

Once free, Aesop is said to have travelled to Athens where he defended the common people against injustice and corruption. His fame, which spread quickly, displeased

Pisistratus the despotic ruler of Athens, to whom free speech was anathema. The old and widely held belief, though, that Aesop was condemned to death for sacrilege and thrown over a cliff, is no longer held with the same certainty it once was.

Without much concrete biographical evidence, it is tempting to conclude that Aesop never actually existed. This conclusion would, though, be as specious as some of the legends that have sprung up around him. Aristophanes, Plato, Zenophon, Aristotle, and Plutarch all make reference to Aesop in their written works – and it is hard to imagine a more impressive group of witnesses to testify he existed. Plato, for example, records that Socrates, while in prison awaiting execution, re-wrote some of Aesop's fables in verse (*Phaedo* 60b).

From fragments of Aristotle's lost *Constitution of Samos*, we learn that Aesop was, in all probability, from Mesembria in Thrace on the Greek mainland and only later lived for some time on the island of Samos. There, Aristotle tells us in his *Rhetoric*, Aesop pleaded for the life of a popular leader before the Samian Assembly, employing his fables to profound effect.

Once free speech was established in Greek cities after Aesop's death, the popularity of his fables increased. In their debates, rhetoricians and scholars often used fables that had been passed on by word of mouth. It was not until around 300 BCE, however, that the first collection of fables, entitled *Assemblies of Aesopic Tales*, appeared in Alexandria Library. Numerous collections have since been made incorporating fables from many sources, in particular from India and Libya. They are all simply referred to as Aesop's fables.

Therefore, this selection undoubtedly contains some fables originating from other minds. While the issue of authorship provides challenges for researchers, the debate itself cements Aesop's pre-eminent position as the father of fable – even though the oral tradition of this literary form reaches back into the mists of time.

THEMATIC KEYWORD INDEX

N.B. Numbers refer to the fable number in this book – they are not page numbers.

A

ABSTINENCE
    increases pleasure on recommencing   94
ACCIDENTS
    hurt less than intentional harm   106
    occur when least expected   113
ACCOMPLICES
    share in a crime, share in the guilt   23
ACTIONS
    convey respect or disrespect   27
    should first be thought through   113
    try using persuasion before resorting to force   48

THEMATIC KEYWORD INDEX

ADULTERY
    will it come to a sticky end?   29
ADVERSITY
    shows the true character of friends and colleagues   35
ADVICE
    don't expect others to accept advice that hasn't worked for you   47
AIDING AND ABETTING
    there's no escape from responsibility   43
ALLIANCES
    fraught if made with recent enemies   71
AMBITIONS
    appropriate ones are more likely to be fulfilled   31
    envy can lead us to have unreasonable aspirations   56
APPEASEMENT
    only increases the enemy's potential for harming   92
APPETITE
    must not be allowed to over-rule reason   37, 42
ARGUMENT
    ineffectual against the irrational   4
ARROGANCE
    blinds us to our weaknesses   15
    may indicate ignorance   69
    thinking you can do anything, either causes embarrassment or harm   42

THEMATIC KEYWORD INDEX

ASSUMPTIONS
    can cause embarrassment   88
    can cause pain   113
AWARENESS
    who's writing or speaking?   2, 30

B

BAD LUCK
    an unhealthy interest in the bad luck of others   66
    calamities are borne more courageously than trifling misfortunes   76
BANKRUPTCY
    more likely if you are over-committed   22
BEAUTY
    the dangers of a shallow interpretation   50
BEHAVIOUR
    expresses our respect for others vividly   27
    the danger of becoming a liar   105
    treat others as you want to be treated   101, 118
    we see our own in others   52
BENEFACTORS
    how not to treat them   98
BETRAYAL
    of others may increase danger to self   28, 64

THEMATIC KEYWORD INDEX

BLAMING
    first, find the reason for the fault   86
    we would rather blame someone else for our foolishness   51

BLESSINGS
    are often overlooked   116
    can only be enjoyed where there's freedom   54

BOASTING
    best cured by testing   10
    by only stressing positive aspects   91
    draws attention to other short-comings   19
    in the absence of a possible contradiction   97
    the dangers of bragging about your wealth   61
    usually points to ignorance   54

BODY
    prized for its beauty, but ultimately it's a tool   50

BOLDNESS
    when is it appropriate?   121

BULLIES
    how they avoid conflict with the strong   65

BUSINESS
    can spoil friendships   8
    don't jeopardize small gains lightly   117
    even when things are going well, remain vigilant   9
    false economies   107

THEMATIC KEYWORD INDEX

BUSINESS (continued)
   good data minimizes risks   32
   how committed are my partners?   58
   likelihood of bankruptcy increases if we are
      over-committed   22
   remain flexible   110
   venturing into new areas is risky   73
   with whom am I dealing? (See INVESTMENT)   28

C

CAMPAIGNING
   the best candidate may not run the best campaign   102
CARELESSNESS
   brought on by over-confidence   15, 113
   brought on by the best of intentions   115
CAUTION
   however desperate the situation, be cautious   37
CHANGE
   assess carefully before acting   83
CHARACTER
   demonstrated by our choice of friends   55
   not judged by great deeds alone   99
   previous good character may not save you if
      crime is serious   23

THEMATIC KEYWORD INDEX

CHARACTER (continued)
 revealed to others in extreme circumstances   35
 rudeness as an all-pervading flaw   89
 some predictions can be made about others by
  knowing their character   49
 the value of being moderate and stable   78

CHARITY
 wasted on the vicious and ungrateful   21

CHILDREN
 not responsible for parents' faults   86

CLAIRVOYANCE
 a practical test   68

CLEVERNESS
 misuse creates a debt   101
 not to be confused with wisdom   39

COMFORT
 taken from seeing others worse off than ourselves   40

COMMITMENT
 essential to successful partnerships   58

COMPATIBILITY
 some differences are too great to overcome   8

COMPETITION
 know who you are up against   9

THEMATIC KEYWORD INDEX

COMPLACENCY
   only gives short-term comfort   70
COMPLAINTS
   one way of handling them   62
   those who complain the loudest, often have the
      least to complain about   38
CONFIDENCE
   without foundation is mere bravado   118
CONFLICTS
   won or deterred by preparedness   87
CONTEMPT
   as a result of familiarity   122
CONTRACTS
   assess fully before committing yourself   71
   don't try to make deals with people whose values
      are quite different to your own (e.g., thieves)   49
   ensure you have a remedy for breaches   7
CONVICTION
   acting boldly   121
CO-OPERATION
   less forthcoming from the powerful   28
   yields efficiency and security   3
COUNSEL
   practical help may be of more use   44

THEMATIC KEYWORD INDEX

COURAGE
    hard to muster in the case of little grievances   76
    has little to do with size   24

COVETOUSNESS
    lack of appreciation of what we already possess   18
    may backfire   72, 80
    those who want everything for themselves, give little to others (see GREED)   60

COWARDICE
    not easily overcome by reasoning   24

CREDIBILITY
    undermined by hollow threats   33

CREDIT
    only to be taken where due   88

CRIME
    parental responsibility   95
    those who encourage others are also culpable   43

CRIMINALS
    their presence increases victims' suffering   79

CRISES
    if you have choices, you still have some control   63
    initially, practical help is more valuable than counsel   44

CRUELTY
    borne of hate and a lack of empathy   53

CUSTOMS
may not serve present needs — 115

D

DANGER
adaptability aids survival — 5, 110
an excellent test of friendship — 35
created by betrayal — 64
lurks where least expected — 9
mitigated by being prepared — 87

DATA
the value of gathering appropriate data — 32

DEALS
check-out parties and costs — 71

DEATH
only welcomed in extreme circumstances — 96
some ways of dying are less desirable than others — 63

DEATH PENALTY
a parent's anguish — 95

DECISIONS
if you're in love, don't make hasty decisions — 20

DECISIVENESS
when it's lacking — 125

THEMATIC KEYWORD INDEX

DEEDS
good ones are long remembered — 85
DEFENCE
is not always confrontational — 110
put what you have to best use — 87
DELUSIONS OF GRANDEUR
dangerous flights of fancy that drag you down lower than when you started — 56
forgetting facts — 123
DESIRABILITY
primarily based on utility and beauty — 12
DESTINY
your actions play a role — 51
DETERMINATION
you're not beaten until you give up — 103
DETERRENCE
the value of being able to strike from a distance — 75
DIETING
not all diets suit all people — 6
DISASTERS
make us start to think about life as a whole — 52
the mistake of thinking they only strike others — 66
DISDAIN
caused by dented pride — 67

THEMATIC KEYWORD INDEX

DISEASE
    how good is the treatment?   124
DISENFRANCHISED
    their situation changes little with a change of government   74
D.I.Y.
    is not always the cheapest option   107
DOMESTIC DISCORD
    making an assessment   89

E

EAGERNESS
    should be tempered by caution   37
ECONOMICS
    some savings come at a high price   107
EFFORT
    the value of doing one's best   85
EGOISM
    causes deafness to the needs of others   90
ELECTIONS
    look beyond the hype   102
EMBARRASSMENT
    caused by accepting praise meant for another   88

THEMATIC KEYWORD INDEX

EMERGENCIES
- the value of being prepared — 87

ENEMIES
- know when to tolerate them — 110
- seek to exploit the differences between allies — 3

ENVY
- can lead us to have unreasonable ambitions — 56
- do you have the whole picture? — 108

EQUALITY
- before the law is one thing, with respect to attributes quite another — 45, 120
- justice cannot be achieved without it — 13

EVIL
- abhorrent in whatever form it takes — 59
- those who encourage evil are guilty, too — 43
- wishing harm on others — 109

EXAMPLE
- more powerful than words — 100

EXCESS
- leads to boredom — 94

EXPECTATION
- expect of yourself what you expect of others — 100

EXPLOITATION
- of benefactors — 98

F

FACTS
   the bedfellows of fiction — 30

FADS
   why they die out — 94

FAILURE
   if you can anticipate it, make contingency plans — 39
   insult is often added to injury — 56

FAME
   or is it just notoriety? — 104

FAMILY
   harmonious co-operation makes it strong — 3

FATE
   not entirely outside our control — 51

FAULTS
   apportioning blame requires care — 86
   why are they easily seen by others? — 57

FEAR
   of the unfamiliar — 122

FICTION
   often paraded as fact — 30

FIRST AID
   the most injured are often the quietest — 38

THEMATIC KEYWORD INDEX

FIRST IMPRESSION
when a show of strength is needed — 75

FLATTERY
flatterers may also be bullies — 65
usually employed for a reason — 84

FLEXIBILITY
aids survival — 110

FOOD
variety ensures continual enjoyment — 94

FOOLISHNESS
blaming others for our carelessness — 51
caused by arrogance and ignorance — 42
caused by being in love — 20
often results from poor timing — 14

FORCE
judicious early use of limited force — 75
may fail where persuasion succeeds — 48
timely use may avoid greater bloodshed — 33

FORESIGHT
acting on it lessens suffering — 11, 87

FORTUNE
are you truly a winner? — 29

FREEDOM
essential to the enjoyment of other blessings — 54

THEMATIC KEYWORD INDEX

FREE-LOADERS
   practitioners encourage others   93
FRIENDSHIP
   could be spoilt by engaging in business   8
   friends can harm each other through ignorance   115
   future value of it is incalculable   1
   is tested by adversity   35
   requires mutual respect   118
   the importance of trust   112
   we are judged by the company we keep   55

G

GAMBLING
   what are your chances?   117
GENEROSITY
   must come out of own pocket   93
   ostentatious generosity may hide meanness   82
GIVING
   quality is more appreciated than quantity   82
   rarely found among the covetous   60
   the exploitation of givers by recipients   98
GOVERNMENTS
   all seem alike to the disenfranchised   74
   should be valued for what they do not do   116

THEMATIC KEYWORD INDEX

GREED
  can you still save yourself?   29
  may cost you what you already possess   18, 72
  taking more than you are given   98
  you may end up with nothing   80

GRIEF
  where blame attaches, vengeance follows   79

H

HABITUATION
  can lead to greater tolerance   62

HAPPINESS
  comes to those who learn from others   77

HARM
  can be done with the best of intentions   115
  much more painful when intentional   106
  when wished upon others   109

HATE
  destroyer of reason   53

HELP
  first, do everything you can yourself   17
  give practical assistance first, counsel later   44
  may have strings attached   114
  not easily obtained by known liars   105

THEMATIC KEYWORD INDEX

HISTORY
    always ask, from whose point of view   30
HOARDING
    a risky practice   81
HONESTY
    the quickest way to the crux of the matter   82
HOPE
    even a shred of hope gives strength   63
    however slight, defies death   96
HYPOCRISY
    the danger of pretending to be what one is not   68

I

IGNORANCE
    can cost a friend dearly   115
    can shield us from harsh realities   54
ILLNESS
    consider all treatments   124
INABILITY
    often blamed on circumstances   67
INDECISIVENESS
    serves no one   125
INFERIORS
    assume equality when you are down   25

THEMATIC KEYWORD INDEX

INFORMATION
   good information allows for good decision-making   32
   some is ignored at your peril   2

INJURIES
   easier to bear if accidental   106
   hard to forget if the perpetrator lives nearby   79

INSULTS
   ask, who's speaking?   111
   very painful when from friends   118

INTEGRITY
   its importance to clients   68

INTELLIGENCE
   lack of it soon shows in politics   102
   more desirable than brawn   69

INTENSIVE FARMING
   have we reaped all the disadvantages yet?   72

INVENTING
   need-driven solutions   103

INVESTMENT
   lavishly advertised opportunities often give poor returns   26
   preferable to hoarding   81
   windows of opportunity   70

INVITATIONS
   should always be from host   93

THEMATIC KEYWORD INDEX

IRRATIONAL BEHAVIOUR
    may be caused by lovesickness   20

J

JUDGEMENTS
    impaired by grief   79
    investigate all angles   123
    the ones we make about others often apply
        to us, too   52
    understand what motivates others   119
JUSTICE
    demands equality before the law   13
    often overridden by gain   90

K

KIDNAPPING
    the unfortunate consequence of meeting demands   92
KINDNESS
    select recipients with care   21
KNOWLEDGE
    not all first-hand knowledge is worth the price
        (see LEARNING)   77

THEMATIC KEYWORD INDEX

L

LATERAL THINKING
    provoking the mind to make creative jumps   103
LAW
    essential for dealing with an anarchic minority
        in the interest of equality and justice   45
LAZINESS
    does not inspire others to help you   17
    expecting others to subsidize your hobbies   11
    the easier way often leads to ruin   39
LEARNING
    life is a harsh teacher   2
    self-preservation learnt from misfortunes of others   77
LEISURE
    very costly when placed before work   11
LIARS
    boasting when there's no danger of contradiction   97
    eventually, bring punishment on themselves   105
LIFESTYLES
    each has its hidden costs and dangers   108
LOSS
    due to bad decisions   95
LOVE
    when you're in love, you lose your head   20

THEMATIC KEYWORD INDEX

LUXURIES
    only valued in times of plenty   12
LYING
    extremely hard to maintain over time   97

M

MATERIALISM
    blinds us to what is important about our nature   50
MEALS
    there's no such thing as a free meal   29
MEDIATION
    the importance of trust and respect   120
MEDICINE
    seek a second opinion   92
    what are the side effects?   124
MIND
    qualities of mind more important than your body   50
MISFORTUNE
    calamities are borne more courageously than trifling misfortunes   76
    danger of taking an unhealthy interest in that of others   66
MISPLACED TRUST
    beware of those who are generous at another's cost   93

THEMATIC KEYWORD INDEX

MISTAKES
    those observed in others can be avoided   2
MODERATION
    closely linked to long-term stability   78
    increases chances of success   80
MONEY
    its true value resides in its use   81
MOTIVATION
    a potent driving force   119

N

NATURE
    does not yield to kindness   21
    sets limits to our activities   31
NECESSITY
    can drive creative thinking   103
NEIGHBOURS
    coping with bad ones   62
NEWNESS
    always exciting   94
NOTORIETY
    fame's poor cousin   104

O

OBSEQUIOUSNESS
  excessive compliance with the wishes of others ... 125
OPINIONS
  dangerous to care too much about
    those of others ... 84, 125
OVER-AMBITIOUSNESS
  can be a hindrance to success ... 80
OVER-CONFIDENCE
  can lead to your downfall ... 15
OVER-REACTING
  invites censure ... 76

P

PAIN
  can result from seeking too much pleasure ... 29
PARANORMAL PRACTITIONERS
  always subjected to severe scrutiny ... 68
PARENTING
  taking responsibility for failure ... 95
PARENTS
  responsible for the faults they pass on ... 86

THEMATIC KEYWORD INDEX

PARTNERSHIPS
    commitment on both sides is essential   58
    evaluated in challenging times   35
    not worth accepting in doomed ventures   71

PEACE
    achieved in countries where justice prevails   13

PEACE ENVOYS
    choosing the right person   120

PERSUASION
    benefits offered must at least appear to exceed the other's costs   63
    fails unless you can appeal to the other's values or self-interest   49
    whenever possible, aim to use the least force   48

PETTINESS
    can be brought on by jealousy   36

PHONINESS
    caused by a thwarted ego   67
    detrimental to friendship   112

PHYSIQUE
    sets limits to certain ambitions   56

PLANNING
    be thorough to avoid negative consequences   29, 39
    some things can be known about the future   11

THEMATIC KEYWORD INDEX

POLITICS
    new is not necessarily better   116
    of little interest to the disenfranchised   74
POMPOSITY
    no guarantee of success   26
POSSESSIONS
    enjoyed by different people in diverse ways   81
POVERTY
    a humble life has some advantages   91
PRACTICAL JOKES
    jokers must expect to become victims themselves   101
PREACHING
    not welcomed from non-practitioners   100
PREDICTIONS
    some can be based on the values of others   49
PRIDE
    can lead to ridiculous behaviour   69
    causes blindness to own weaknesses   78
    dangerous when indulged in for the wrong reasons   41
    humiliation leads to negative emotions   67
PRIVILEGES
    always come at a price   108
PROFESSIONALISM
    lack of integrity invites censure   47, 68

PROFIT
    often at the expense of justice or other people   90
    what's the gamble?   117
PROJECTION
    blaming others for our faults   16
PROMISES
    beneficial to both parties when kept   1
    not to be made rashly   22
PROOF
    when its absence points to the truth   97
PROPRIETY
    gives you greater dignity   14
PRUDENCE
    much the safer way to proceed   32
PUNISHMENT
    needs to be appropriate and timely   95
    of those aiding and abetting   43
    of those maltreating benefactors   98

Q

QUACKERY
    exposed by partial knowledge and a lack of integrity   47

THEMATIC KEYWORD INDEX

QUALITY
    always appreciated, often of greater importance
        than quantity   34
QUANTITY
    a poor substitute for quality   34
QUARRELLING
    best done in private   25
QUESTIONS
    ask the wrong question, get the wrong answer   6

R

REASON
    a poor tool with which to instil courage   24
    destroyed by hate   53
    the constant battle with appetites   37
RELIABILITY
    can compensate for lack of speed   15
REPUTATION
    the better, the greater the downfall   91
RESPECT
    best shown while the person is alive   27
    integrity is a prerequisite   99
RESPONSIBILITY
    aiding and abetting   43

THEMATIC KEYWORD INDEX

REVENGE
    too personal and disproportionate, may backfire   53
    usually comes at a high price   114
REVOLUTION
    assess any potential drawbacks   83
RIDICULE
    poured on those who quarrel in public   25
    visited on the arrogant who fail   102
RIGHT AND WRONG
    a parent's failure to teach this   95
RISKS
    assess before acting   117
    minimized by accurate information   32
    not worth taking where there is nothing to gain   2
RUBBERNECKING
    the inherent risk   66
RUDENESS
    occasional or character trait?   89

S

SABRE-RATTLING
    a willingness to act is essential to future credibility   33
SACRIFICES
    readily made for love   20

THEMATIC KEYWORD INDEX

SCHADENFREUDE
   taking pleasure in the misfortunes of others
      often backfires   66
SCHOLARS
   respect for them diminished by foolishness   99
SCORN
   for intellectuals who fail to tie their shoelaces   99
SECURITY
   do not draw attention to your wealth   81
SELF-AWARENESS
   accept your limitation   6, 42
   understand other people's perceptions of yourself   5
   why our faults are hard to see   57
SELF-ESTEEM
   don't try to be something you're not   6
   over-confidence can lead to a kick in the teeth   46
   over-rating yourself can lead to setbacks   56
   re-evaluate your strengths   40, 41
SELFISHNESS
   often overrides justice   90
   the worst kind   36
SELF-PRESERVATION
   learnt from the fate of others   77

THEMATIC KEYWORD INDEX

SELF-WORTH
make yourself valuable by seeking an environment
   in which you can shine   41
SENSITIVITY
over-sensitivity to the opinions of others   125
SHOPAHOLICS
as soon as you possess the item, it loses some of
   its attraction ... and the money is gone   73
SHORTCOMINGS
exposed by bragging   19
SHORTSIGHTEDNESS
choosing short-term advantages to your detriment   70
SHOUTING
those who shout the most, often have the least
   to offer   26
SHOWING-OFF
only makes you look less impressive   19
SIZE
bigger is not necessarily better   1
not an indicator of courage   24
SKILL
there's always more to a simple task than meets
   the eye   46
SMELLS
acquired tolerance for bad ones   62

THEMATIC KEYWORD INDEX

SOCIALISING
    treat others as you would like to be treated   101
SOUR GRAPES
    inability to cope with failure   67
SPEAKING
    think first   84
STATUS
    diminished by over-familiarity with inferiors   122
    must be earned (or inherited?), can't be borrowed   118
STEALING
    an inappropriate way to salve your conscience   82
    condoning leads to an escalation of crime   95
STICKYBEAKS
    much encouraged by public quarrels   25
STINGINESS
    unlikely to increase your gains   107
STRENGTH
    achieved through co-operation   3
    comes in various guises   110
    depends on circumstances   1, 111
STUBBORNNESS
    a lack of insight   70
SUCCESS
    moderation increases your chances   80

SUFFERING
    getting a new perspective on it can be helpful   40
    hard to gauge from what the sufferer says   38
    re-lived when the victim is reminded of incident   79

SUICIDE
    stop: seek help; others have come through similar situations   40

SURRENDER
    know when to give a little to survive   77, 110

SURVIVAL
    everyone's a potential rescuer   1, 105
    know when to go with the flow   110
    the value of adaptability   5, 77

T

TACTICS
    must suit circumstances   5

TALENT
    on its own does not guarantee success   15

TEACHING
    best achieved by example   100

TENACITY
    can compensate for a lack of talent   15

THEMATIC KEYWORD INDEX

THREATS
    are as powerful as the person who makes them   9
    be prepared to back them up with action   33
    powerful when accompanied by limited action   75

TIMING
    poor timing makes you look foolish   11, 14

TOLERANCE
    developed through habituation   62

TRADES
    safer to stick with what you are trained in   46

TRAITORS
    become despised by all and are exposed to great danger   28, 64

TRUST
    must be earned   58
    the hallmark of friendship   112

TRUTH
    its habit of emerging eventually   97
    look at all sides   123
    often painful and costly to ascertain   22

TYRANNY
    despots can always find excuses for it   4
    only fools trust tyrants   28

THEMATIC KEYWORD INDEX

U

UNFAIRNESS
    exacerbated by power inequality   77
UNGRATEFULNESS
    to be expected from the vicious   21
UNIONISM
    the strength of the collective voice and deed   3
UNITY
    yields strength and security   3

W

WAIT-AND-SEE MENTALITY
    unable to cope with emergencies   87
WANTING
    what we haven't got always seems so desirable   73
WARFARE
    the deterrent value of a long-distance strike capability   75
WEALTH
    a liability if poorly managed   61
    brings with it worries and dangers   81, 91

THEMATIC KEYWORD INDEX

WEALTH (continued)
 enriching yourself often puts you in competition
  with others   9
WELFARE STATE
 must take some responsibility for encouraging
  dependency   86
WELTANSCHAUUNG
 determines how we react to calamities   52
WILFULNESS
 flying in the face of reason   70
WISDOM
 a combination of intelligence and experience   2
WISHES
 the danger of unreasonable ones   31
WORK
 know your employer   7
 seasonal work cannot be postponed   11
 seek work that values your strengths   41
 work with a will (see BUSINESS)   121

AESOP'S FABLES

1 THE LION AND THE MOUSE

A lion became angry when a mouse woke him by running across his face.

"Please don't kill me," begged the mouse, "one day I will be able to help you."

The lion gave a scornful laugh and let him go.

Not long afterwards, some hunters caught the lion and bound him with strong ropes. The mouse heard his roar, found him, and gnawed through the ropes.

"You laughed at the idea of me helping you," said the mouse, "but now you know that even a mouse can be of help to a lion."

The value of friends cannot be judged by their size.

2 THE SICK LION

Too weak to hunt, an old lion lay down in his den and announced to all who passed that he was sick. Many animals came to express their sorrow at his ill health, and each one became another meal.

After many animals had disappeared in this way, the fox realized what the trick was. He positioned himself outside the den and inquired how the lion was.

"Not too good," replied the lion, "but do come in and talk with me."

The fox stayed where he was and replied:

"No, thank you. I can see many footprints made by visitors entering your den, however, I see none from any leaving."

The wise learn from the mistakes of others.

3   THE FATHER AND HIS SONS

A father became tired of the endless quarrelling between his sons. When all his efforts to reconcile them failed, he told them to bring him a bundle of sticks. He then asked each one in turn to try to break the whole bundle in half. Each tried as hard as he could but was unable to break it. The father then untied the bundle and gave each son one stick. These they snapped with ease.

"You see," said the father, "if you work together, you will be like the unbreakable bundle of sticks. But if you are divided, if you quarrel and fight among yourselves, then your enemies will destroy you as easily as you broke these sticks."

There is strength in unity.

4   THE WOLF AND THE LAMB

A wolf met a lamb that had strayed from the flock. Instead of simply attacking him, the wolf decided to justify to the lamb why he had a right to eat him.

"Last year you insulted me!" said the wolf.

"Last year," said the lamb meekly, "I wasn't even born."

"Well," retorted the wolf, "you eat the grass in my field!"

"That's not true," replied the lamb, "I am too young to eat grass."

"All right, then," snapped the wolf, "you drink from my well!"

"No," cried the lamb, "my mother's milk is my food and drink."

When he heard this, the wolf ate the lamb, saying:

"Did you really think I was going to go without my supper, just because you deny every one of my accusations?"

A tyrant will always find an excuse for tyranny.

5 THE BAT AND THE WEASELS

A bat fell to the ground and was caught by a weasel. The bat pleaded for his life, but the weasel said that he was the natural enemy of all birds. The bat convinced the weasel that he was not a bird, but a mouse, and his life was spared.

Not long afterwards, the bat once again fell to the ground and was caught by another weasel. This weasel said he loved eating mice. The bat begged the weasel not to eat him, as he was a bat and not a mouse. Once again, he escaped death.

The wise use circumstances to their advantage.

6 THE DONKEY AND THE GRASSHOPPERS

A donkey fell in love with the chirping of some grasshoppers. When he asked them what they ate to give them such charming voices, they replied:

"Oh, just dew."

The donkey immediately changed his diet and died soon afterwards.

A vain pursuit coupled with ignorance is a recipe for disaster.

7 THE WOLF AND THE CRANE

A wolf promised to pay a crane a generous sum of money if she would put her head into his throat and pull out a bone that had got stuck there. She performed the operation and asked for the payment. The wolf grinned, ground his teeth, and said:

"Surely, escaping with your life, after putting your head in a wolf's mouth, is payment enough!"

> *If you work for the wicked do not expect rewards*
> *– you will be lucky to escape unharmed.*

8   THE CHARCOAL BURNER AND THE FULLER*

A charcoal burner who used his house for his work said to his friend:

"Why don't you come and live with me? We would both save on household expenses."

His friend, who was a fuller, answered:

"That would be impossible, for you would blacken my wool cloth with your charcoal, just as soon as I get it clean and white."

Like attracts like.

---

* A fuller finishes wool cloth by scouring and thickening it.

9   THE BOY HUNTING LOCUSTS

A boy hunting for locusts had caught quite a few when a scorpion appeared before him. Mistaking him for just another locust, he stretched out his hand. The scorpion waved his sting in the air and said:

"If you'd touched me, boy, you'd have lost me and your locusts!"

> *The seriousness of a threat is directly proportional to its capacity to be carried out.*

10 THE BOASTING TRAVELLER

On his return home, a traveller boasted about heroic deeds he had performed abroad. Apart from other astounding things he had done, he bragged that at Rhodes he had leapt further than any other man of his day could leap – and that many people had seen him do it and could affirm the truth of his claim.

"Well, that's wonderful," interrupted a shrewd bystander, "but we don't need any witnesses: just imagine this is Rhodes and show us your leap!"

The best way to cure someone of boasting is to set a test.

11   THE ANTS AND THE GRASSHOPPER

On a bright winter's day, a starving grasshopper came across some ants drying grain harvested in the summer. When he begged for a little food, the ants asked:

"Why didn't you store some food during the summer?"

"Oh," he answered sadly, "I was far too busy singing all day."

On hearing this, the ants said scornfully:

"If you sing all day in the summer, you'll have to dance on an empty stomach in the winter."

Laziness leads to need.

12 THE COCK AND THE JEWEL

A cock was scratching for food for himself and his hens when he found a precious stone.

"If your owner had found you," he crowed, "you'd be valued. As for me, I'd rather have one grain of barley than a whole crown studded with jewels!"

The value of an article is its desirability.

13   THE KINGDOM OF THE LION

A wise lion ruled over the animals of field and forest. He was never wrathful, cruel, or tyrannical, but always just and gentle. During his reign, he proclaimed that he would found a general assembly of all the animals, in which the wolf and the lamb, the tiger and the stag, the panther and the kid, and the dog and the hare, would all live together in peace and friendship.

"Oh, how long have I dreamt of the day," said the hare, "when the weak will be able to take their place in safety by the side of the strong."

Only where there is justice can the meek live in peace.

14   THE FISHERMAN PIPING

A fisherman, who was also an able musician, took his flute and his nets to the sea. He found a projecting rock, spread out his nets on it, and began to play. He played several tunes, hoping the fish, attracted by the music, would voluntarily jump into his nets. When after a long time nothing happened, he put down his flute, cast his net into the sea and hauled in a large catch.

"Oh, you crazy creatures," he shouted at the fish, seeing them leaping about in the net on the rock, "when I played my flute you wouldn't dance, but now that I've stopped, you dance so merrily!"

It is hard to do the right thing at the right time.

15   THE HARE AND THE TORTOISE

One day a hare poked fun at the short legs and slow pace of a tortoise. The tortoise just laughed and said:

"You can run like the wind; however, in a race, I will beat you."

The hare thought this was impossible and accepted the challenge, agreeing that the fox should choose the starting post and the finishing post.

On the day of the race, they started together. The tortoise did not stop once. He just kept going at his slow but steady pace all the way to the finishing post. The hare, confident of his ability to outrun the tortoise, took a little rest along the way and fell fast asleep. When he at last woke up, he sprinted as fast as he could, only to find the tortoise had already beaten him to the finishing post.

Slow and steady wins the race.

16   THE TRAVELLER AND HIS DOG

A traveller was about to set off on a journey when he saw his dog stretching himself.

"What are you waiting for," he shouted at the dog, "let's get going."

The dog wagged his tail and said:

"I've been ready all along; I'm just waiting for you."

A loiterer often blames his efficient friends for delays.

17   HERCULES AND THE WAGONER

A carter was driving his bullock-drawn wagon down a country lane when the wheels sank into a deep rut. The driver, a simple man, just stood helplessly next to his wagon calling to Hercules for help. It is said that Hercules appeared and told the driver:

"Put your shoulders to those wheels; coax your beasts to pull harder. Don't pray to me for help until you've done your best to help yourself, or else your prayers will fall on deaf ears."

The best help is self-help.

18   THE DOG AND HIS REFLECTION

A dog was crossing a bridge with a large piece of meat in his mouth. In the water, he saw his reflection. Mistaking his reflection for another dog with a larger piece of meat, he immediately attacked him, hoping to gain a second piece of meat for himself. As he did so, his own piece of meat floated away down the river and the other dog's larger piece of meat vanished.

Covetousness detracts from what we already possess.

19   THE MOLE AND HIS MOTHER

A young mole boasted to his mother:

"Unlike other moles, I can see!"

To show him he was mistaken, the mother placed some frankincense in front of him and asked him what it was. The young mole answered confidently:

"It's a pebble!"

The mother cried out in alarm:

"Oh, my son, you're not only blind, but you've lost your sense of smell!"

Bragging tends to reveal further defects.

20   THE LION IN LOVE

A lion asked a woodcutter for his daughter's hand in marriage. The woodcutter, who was very afraid of the lion, could not simply say no. Instead, he said:

"Yes, but only on one condition. As my daughter is terrified of you, you must allow me to extract your teeth and cut off your claws."

The lovesick lion readily agreed to this, but as soon as he had been rendered harmless, the woodcutter attacked him with a stick and drove him away from his house.

Love swells the heart but clouds our reasoning.

21 THE FARMER AND THE SNAKE

A farmer found a half-frozen snake on a bleak winter's day. He took pity on it and placed it under his tunic to warm it. No sooner had it thawed, than its instincts drove it to bite the farmer. With his dying breath, the farmer gasped:
 "It serves me right for pitying the vicious."

Kindness is wasted on the vicious and ungrateful.

22 THE HERDSMAN AND THE LOST CALF

After much fruitless searching for a lost calf, a herdsman promised to sacrifice a lamb to Hermes, Pan, and the Guardian Deities of the forest, if he could just find out who had stolen his calf. It was not long before he came across the thief, a lion, feeding on the calf's carcass. In terror, he called out to the Guardian Deities of the forest:

"A moment ago, I was willing to offer a lamb to find out who had robbed me, now I'd happily sacrifice a full-grown bull to escape safely from the lion!"

If we had to fulfil all our rash promises,
we would soon be bankrupt.

23   THE FARMER AND THE STORK

A farmer, protecting his newly sown fields, caught several cranes in his nets. Among them, he found one stork whose leg had been fractured by the net.

"Please spare me," begged the stork, "have pity on me, for my leg is broken. Let me go free. I am not a crane, but a stork of excellent character. I am devoted to the care of my parents, and my feathers are nothing like those of these cranes."

"That may all be true," said the farmer, laughing, "however, I have caught you along with these robbers, the cranes, and with them you must die."

Birds of a feather flock together.

24 THE FAWN AND HIS MOTHER

"Why are you so frightened of the hounds?" asked a fawn of its mother. "Aren't you larger and faster, and don't you have antlers with which to defend yourself?"

"What you say is true, my son," replied the deer, "yet I only need to hear the bark of one dog to feel faint and run away as fast as I can."

Reasoning fails to give courage to cowards.

25   THE POMEGRANATE, APPLE TREE, AND BRAMBLE

An apple tree and a pomegranate were arguing over who produced the best fruit when a nearby bramble raised its voice to say:

"Oh, do let's stop quarrelling amongst ourselves!"

> *Quarrelling in public invites your inferiors to assume the right to comment and interfere.*

26   THE MOUNTAIN IN LABOUR

One day, a crowd of people gathered at the foot of a mountain. Strange groans and loud noises had been heard coming from inside it. The people waited in terror, expecting a catastrophe of some kind, when out popped a little mouse.

Do not shout about a small matter: a great start is often followed by an inferior performance.

27 THE BEAR AND THE FOX

A bear boasted of his profound respect for humans, saying that he would not dream of touching a corpse. Hearing this, a fox said:

"I would be far more impressed to hear that you no longer eat them alive!"

Our actions, rather than our words,
manifest respect for others.

28   THE ASS, THE FOX, AND THE LION

An ass and a fox made a pact for their mutual benefit: from now on they would hunt together. They had not been out long when they saw a lion. The fox went up to the lion to broker a deal to save his own life. The fox offered to help the lion catch the ass in return for his word that he would not be harmed. The lion readily agreed, and the fox tricked the ass and caught him in a deep pit.

When the lion saw that the ass had been trapped, he attacked the fox and ate the ass later at his leisure.

Tyrants will co-operate only as far as it suits them.

29 THE FLIES AND THE HONEY POT

A spilt pot of honey attracted several flies that landed in it and ate greedily. Gradually their feet and wings became so covered in honey that they could not escape and suffocated.

"Oh, how stupid we have been," they wailed just before dying. "For a little pleasure, we have destroyed ourselves."

Some pleasures are not worth the cost.

30   THE MAN AND THE LION

Travelling together through the forest, a man and a lion boasted to each other of their respective superiority. As they were arguing they passed a statue of a man strangling a lion.

"You see," said the man, "we can even overpower beasts with our bare hands!"

The lion pointed out that if lions could make statues, the man would be under the lion's paw!

One story may pale when another is told.

31 THE TORTOISE AND THE EAGLE

A tortoise complained that hers was a hard fate. An eagle hovering overhead asked her what reward she would give him if he floated her in the air. She promised him all the riches of the Red Sea, and the eagle agreed to teach her to fly. The eagle, holding her in his talons, flew higher and higher, almost to the clouds, but then let her fall and smash to pieces on a craggy mountain. As the tortoise lay dying she exclaimed:

"I deserve this end. What business have I flying about in the sky when I can scarcely walk on the earth?"

If all our wishes were granted, we would suffer many accidents.

32 THE FOX AND THE GOAT

A fox had fallen down a well and become trapped. When a thirsty goat arrived to take a drink, the fox concealed his plight and said the water was outstanding and encouraged the goat to come down the well. The goat thought only of his thirst and jumped into the well. When the goat had quenched his thirst, he realized they were both trapped. He agreed to place his forelegs on the well wall and let the fox run up his back to escape, having been assured by the fox that he would return to rescue him later. However, once the fox was free, he ran off. The goat complained bitterly at this breach of their bargain, but the fox merely shouted back to him:

"If you had any sense, you would have inspected the way out before going down; you would not have exposed yourself to a danger from which you cannot escape."

Look before you leap.

33 THE FARMER AND THE CRANES

Having sown a field with wheat, a farmer managed to scare off hungry cranes by brandishing an empty sling. However, when they realized that the sling was empty, the cranes returned. Determined to protect his future crop, the farmer loaded his sling with stones and killed many of the birds. The survivors flew off crying to each other:

"This man is no longer just threatening us but starts to show us what he can do."

If words are not enough, back them up with action.

34 THE LIONESS

A group of wild animals were arguing among themselves. They could not decide who should get the most credit for giving birth to the greatest number of young in one pregnancy. In the end, they decided to ask the lioness:

"And how many cubs do you give birth to at a time?" they inquired of her.

"Me?" she laughed, "I give birth to just one cub, but that one is a lion"*

The value is in the quality, not the quantity.

---

* The obvious biological inaccuracy will long have gone unnoticed outside Africa – and does little to lessen the impact of this fable.

35   THE BEAR AND THE TWO TRAVELLERS

Two men were travelling together when suddenly a bear appeared in front of them. One man quickly climbed up a nearby tree. The other, knowing he was about to be attacked and that he could not fight the bear on his own, pretended to be dead. He held his breath while the bear sniffed him inquisitively. The bear did not harm him and soon went on his way. The other man came down from his tree and asked jokingly what the bear had whispered in his friend's ear.

"You might not want to hear this," said the man who had narrowly escaped death, "but he gave me some good advice: Never travel with a friend who deserts you at the first whiff of danger."

Nothing assesses the quality of friendship like adversity.

36   THE DOG IN THE MANGER

A dog lay in a manger and prevented the oxen from eating the hay by snapping and snarling.

"What a selfish dog!" said one ox to the others, "he can't eat the hay himself, nor will he allow those who can."

> *Depriving others of things, just because we cannot enjoy them ourselves, is unacceptable.*

37 THE THIRSTY PIGEON

A very thirsty pigeon saw a glass of water painted on a signboard. Not realizing that it was only a picture, she flew towards it with great speed. On hitting the sign hard, she broke both wings. Unable to fly, she was caught by a passer-by.

Eagerness should not outrun caution.

38   THE OXEN AND THE AXLES

A team of oxen was hauling a very heavy load along a country lane. The wheels groaned and creaked as they turned on their axles.

"What gives you the right to make so much noise?" the oxen said to the wheels. "We're the ones doing all the work – we should be moaning and groaning, not you!"

Those who are genuinely suffering complain the least.

39   THE WOLF IN SHEEP'S CLOTHING

A wolf decided to disguise himself as a sheep to make a comfortable living. He grazed with a flock of sheep and even managed to fool the shepherd. In the evening, the wolf and the flock of sheep were shut up in the fold. That night the shepherd came to fetch a sheep for slaughter. Thinking he had a sheep in his grasp, he killed the wolf.

Harm seeks harm.

40 THE HARES AND THE FROGS

Some hares had become so depressed with their timidity and a life lived in constant danger that they decided to commit suicide by drowning themselves in a deep lake. As they ran towards the lake, confident that death was preferable to the miserable lives they led, they startled some frogs resting at the water's edge. When the hares saw the fear with which the frogs leapt into the water, one of them cried:

"Stop, friends, stop! Life can't be all that bad for us; here are creatures who are even more easily frightened than us!"

There is always someone worse off.

41 THE STAG AT THE POOL

On a sweltering day, a thirsty stag came to a pool to drink. He looked at his reflection and admired the size and shape of his antlers. Then he looked at his slim, weak feet and felt angry and disappointed with himself.

While he was lost in thought, a lion appeared at the pool and prepared to pounce on him. As quick as lightning, the stag sped across the plain on his swift feet – easily outrunning the lion. But then he came to a dense forest and his magnificent antlers became entangled in the low branches of a tree. When the lion caught him by the throat, he reproached himself bitterly:

"All my life I have deceived myself. I despised the feet that might have saved me and took immense pride in the antlers that are my death sentence."

Truly valuable attributes are often overlooked.

42   THE DOGS AND THE HIDES

A pack of starving dogs saw some cowhides that a skinner had left at the bottom of a stream. As they could not reach them, they decided to drink up the water. Unfortunately, they burst themselves long before they got anywhere near the hides.

Do not attempt the impossible.

43 THE TRUMPETER TAKEN PRISONER

A captured trumpeter, who had been bravely leading his soldiers, begged his enemy to spare his life:

"I haven't killed a single man of your troop, nor do I carry arms. All I carry is this harmless trumpet." To this his captor replied:

"And that is precisely why you should die. You don't fight yourself, but with your trumpet, you rouse your men to do battle."

He who does something through another does it himself.

44 THE BOY BATHING

A drowning boy called out to a passer-by:
"Help me, please!"
The passer-by, instead of reaching out to help the boy, gave him a lecture on the dangers of swimming in rivers. The boy begged the passer-by to rescue him now and save the wise counsel for later.

Counsel without practical help is useless in a crisis.

45   THE HARES AND THE LIONS

The hares addressed the assembly, pleading most earnestly that all animals should be equal. In response, the lions said:
"Your words, honourable hares, are fine words indeed, but they lack the claws and teeth that ours have."

Without a constitution and laws,
equality is but a pipe dream.

46 THE ASS AND THE WOLF

An ass pretended to be lame when he saw a wolf stalking him. The wolf, who no longer saw any urgency to kill the ass, asked about his lameness. The ass told him that a thorn had become lodged in his hoof and that he had better remove it before eating him.

The wolf thought that this was a sensible idea and examined the hoof carefully. Suddenly, the ass kicked violently, sending the wolf's teeth down his throat. In a terrible state, the wolf moaned:

"This serves me right; I had no business playing the part of a healer when all my father taught me was how to be a butcher."

Stick with what you know.

47 THE QUACK FROG

A frog emerged from his home in the marshes and announced to all beasts, great and small, that he was a learned doctor, highly skilled in the use of medicines and able to cure all manner of diseases.

A wily fox asked him:

"How can you cure others when you can't even cure your own lameness and wrinkled skin?"

> *Physician, heal yourself! Only satisfactory results convince others of one's abilities.*

48   THE NORTH WIND AND THE SUN

The north wind and the sun were arguing about who was the more powerful. It was agreed that whoever managed to strip the clothes off a wayfarer would be the victor. The north wind blew as hard as he could, but the man only wrapped his clothes more tightly around himself. Eventually, the north wind gave up and it was the sun's turn.

As soon as the man felt the warm rays on his back, he stripped off one layer after another. Finally, he was quite naked and had to bathe himself in a nearby stream to cool off.

Persuasion is better than force.

49   THE THIEVES AND THE COCK

Some thieves broke into a house but found nothing but a cock to steal. When they got home, and were preparing to kill the cock, he pleaded for his life:

"Please don't kill me: I am extremely useful! I wake everyone up before it is light so that they can start their day's work on time." To this, the thieves replied angrily:

"That is exactly why we must kill you. When you wake all the neighbours with your crowing, our night's business ends."

The safeguarding of virtue is of no interest to the wicked.

50 THE FOX AND THE LEOPARD

The fox and the leopard were arguing over who was the most beautiful. The leopard boasted about the varied spots that adorned his skin.

"That may be so," interrupted the fox, "but I am still more beautiful than you, for I have a varied and decorated mind."

Qualities of mind and spirit are of greater value than a beautiful body.

51 THE TRAVELLER AND FORTUNE

An exhausted traveller lay down on the wall of a well to have a sleep. Just as he was about to slip off and fall down the well, Dame Fortune came to him.

"Wake up!" she said firmly. "If you had fallen down the well, I would have got a bad name among mortals. I am forever being blamed for the calamities people suffer – even for those that they have brought upon themselves through foolishness."

To a significant extent, we are masters of our fate.

52 THE PHILOSOPHER, THE ANTS, AND MERCURY

A philosopher reproached providence on seeing a shipwreck from which there were no survivors.

"Surely, even if there was perhaps one criminal on board, it can't be right for all the other innocent people to die as well?"

As he was pondering the apparent injustice of the situation, an ant stung him. Finding himself surrounded by an army of ants, he immediately trampled them all to death. Suddenly, Mercury appeared and struck him with his wand:

"And who are you to judge providence? You have just treated these ants in much the same way!"

Take a close look at your own behaviour before judging that of others.

53   THE FARMER AND THE FOX

Having lost many chickens, a farmer built up much hatred towards a fox. When the farmer finally caught the fox, he was determined to exact revenge. He tied some flax soaked in oil to the fox's tail and set it alight. The terrified fox fled through the wheat fields. The farmer, who had been about to harvest the wheat, watched as his entire crop turned to ash. He returned home, bitterly regretting his actions.

Revenge is likely to backfire.

54 THE DOVE AND THE CROW

A caged dove was boasting of the considerable number of chicks she had reared. A crow heard her and said:

"My dear friend, stop your unreasonable boasting! The larger your family, the greater is your sorrow at seeing them imprisoned in this cage."

Without freedom, we cannot enjoy our blessings.

55 THE ASS AND HIS PURCHASER

The owner of an ass agreed to let a man try the animal before deciding whether to purchase him. The man took the ass home and put him with all his other asses. The ass immediately joined the laziest and greediest ass in the drove. The man returned the ass without delay.

"But how can you have tried him so fast?" inquired the owner. The man replied simply:

"Oh, that's easy. I know he would be just like the ass of mine that he chose for his companion."

You can know much about others by the company they keep.

56   THE EAGLE AND THE CROW

A crow was overly impressed when he saw an eagle swoop down and carry off a lamb in his talons. He was very envious of the eagle's prize and determined to do the same. He flew up high with a great whirr of his wings and swooped down onto a large ram. By the time he discovered that he was unable to fly off with his prey, his claws had become tangled in the ram's fleece. The shepherd caught him, clipped his wings, and gave him to his children. The children asked excitedly what kind of bird he was:

"He's just a poor crow," answered the shepherd, "but he will tell you that he is an eagle."

Sometimes our ambitions are greater than our powers.

57 THE TWO BAGS

According to an ancient legend, we are all born with two bags hanging from our necks. A small bag hangs in front and is full of our neighbours' faults; a large bag hangs down behind and is filled with our own faults. This shows why we are so quick to find fault with others but fail to see the numerous faults we have ourselves.

We are quick to notice the faults of others
but are blind to our own.

58   THE LION AND THE EAGLE

An eagle flew down and asked a lion to go into partnership with him. The lion answered by saying:

"It sounds like a promising idea, but I need some kind of guarantee. I find it hard to trust you as a friend; you can fly away from your side of the bargain at any time."

Test before you trust.

59 THE FLEA AND THE MAN

On catching a flea, who had annoyed him very much, a man said:

"How dare you feed on my limbs and give me so much trouble to catch you?" The flea answered saying:

"Kind Sir, please spare my life, for I can do you very little harm." The man gave a derisory laugh:

"Now I will certainly kill you, for no evil, irrespective of whether it is small or large, should be tolerated."

Evil should be dealt with on principle.

60   THE VIPER AND THE FILE

A viper entered a blacksmith's forge and asked the tools for food. When he spoke to the file it replied:

"You are a simpleton. No one expects to get anything from me; I only take and never give anything back."

The covetous make poor givers.

61 THE MULES AND THE ROBBERS

Two heavily laden mules trudged along the road. One mule, whose panniers were filled with treasure, held his head up proudly and rang the bells around his neck loudly. The other mule, whose panniers were full of grain, followed in a quiet, humble manner.

Suddenly, robbers ambushed them. In the skirmish between their owners and the robbers, the mule carrying the treasure was wounded. The robbers took all the treasure but ignored the grain. The wounded mule complained bitterly. The other answered:

"I'm glad I wasn't worth robbing! I've lost nothing, and I've not been injured either."

The more you have, the more you stand to lose.

62   THE RICH MAN AND THE TANNER

A rich man, who could not bear the unpleasant smells his neighbour made, tried to pressure him to move elsewhere. The neighbour, a tanner, always said that he would be moving soon but never actually left.

As time passed, the rich man became accustomed to the smell and complained less frequently, and eventually ceased to complain at all.

One can get used to almost anything.

63   THE LAMB AND THE WOLF

A lamb, who was being chased by a wolf, found safety in a temple. The wolf tried to coax him out.

"If the priest finds you," warned the wolf, "he'll kill and sacrifice you for sure." To this, the lamb replied:

"Getting caught is not a certainty; besides, it would be preferable to being eaten by you!"

Where there is life, there is hope.

64 THE PARTRIDGE AND THE FOWLER

A fowler was about to kill a partridge he had caught when it began to plead for its life:

"Please let me live. If you do, I will act as a decoy and entice many partridges to come to you." To this the fowler replied:

"Now I feel even less hesitation in taking your life, for you would happily betray your friends and relatives to save your own neck!"

Those who betray friends place themselves in great danger.

65 THE CROW AND THE SHEEP

An annoying crow seated himself on a sheep's back. For a long time, the sheep carried the crow around wherever she went. Finally, she plucked up the courage and said:

"If you did this to a dog, you'd soon get to feel its teeth."

To this, the crow answered bluntly:

"I despise the weak but give way to the strong. I know whom I can bully, and whom I must flatter. In this way, I shall live to a ripe old age."

Bullies exploit the weak and flatter the strong.

66   THE SPARROW AND THE HARE

A hare, caught in the strong grasp of an eagle, sobbed and wailed at her fate. A sparrow, on hearing the child-like cries, reproached the hare:

"Of what use are your swift feet now? Why were you so slow?"

While the sparrow was speaking, a hawk swooped down and killed him. The hare took comfort from the sparrow's death, and with her last breath said:

"Well, now you too have suffered a similar calamity - you who thought yourself so safe and took such pleasure in my demise!"

Those who delight in the misfortunes of others are likely to become casualties themselves.

67   THE FOX AND THE GRAPES

A hungry fox saw some bunches of ripe black grapes hanging from a tall, trellised vine. She tried everything she could think of to get them but only succeeded in making herself tired. Finally, she gave up and went away muttering to herself:

"Oh well, who cares? They were sour grapes, anyway."

It is easy to despise what is beyond our grasp.

68   THE PROPHET

A man who claimed he could see into the future sat in a marketplace and told people's fortunes. Suddenly, a stranger ran up to him and announced breathlessly that the fortune teller's house had been broken into and that all his possessions were being stolen. On hearing this, the fortune teller jumped up and ran home as fast as he could.

"Oh, you hypocrite!" shouted one of his neighbours. "You claim to see the future of others but can't even see your own."

The more you claim about yourself, the greater the number of pitfalls.

69   THE WOLF AND THE FOX

One day a wolf was born who was bigger and faster than any of his pack. The other wolves all called him 'Lion.' Unfortunately, his intelligence did not match his size and he took his nickname too seriously. He started to spend all his time with lions. Seeing this, an old sly fox said to him:

"I hope I never make myself look so ridiculous! You've let pride get the better of you. Among wolves, you did appear to be a lion, but among the lions, you are a mere wolf."

Greatness is relative.

70 THE TWO FROGS

Of two frogs who were neighbours, one lived in a deep pond in the countryside, the other in a shallow gully that ran across a nearby road. The frog who lived in the pond said to his friend:

"You really should move. Come and live with me; it would be so much safer for you." But the other frog shook his head:

"I really couldn't," he said, "I've grown so used to my place."

A few days later he was crushed to death under the wheels of a wagon.

The wilful will have their way even at great expense to themselves.

71 THE HARES AND THE FOXES

The hares were at war with the eagles and called to the foxes for help.

"We might have helped you," replied the foxes, "if we didn't know you or your enemy."

Weigh the costs before committing yourself.

72   THE WOMAN AND HER HEN

A woman owned a healthy hen that laid one egg every day. She often thought to herself that there must be a way to get the hen to lay two eggs a day. She decided to feed the hen on double the amount of barley. But instead of achieving the desired outcome, the hen became fat and lazy and stopped laying eggs altogether.

Covetousness is likely to backfire.

73 THE KITES AND THE SWANS

Long ago, both kites and swans were able to sing. The kites, though, on hearing the neighing of horses, were so impressed by the sound that they attempted to copy them. In this way, they lost their ability to sing.

Attempting to gain imaginary benefits often results in the loss of present advantages.

74   THE ASS AND THE OLD SHEPHERD

An ass was quietly feeding in a meadow. Suddenly, his master, the shepherd, ran up to him:

"Please," begged the shepherd, "carry me off as fast as you can - I hear my enemies approaching." The ass looked up from his grazing and replied slowly:

"Why? What's in it for me? Do you think your enemies would ask me to carry two sets of panniers?" The shepherd had to admit that this was very unlikely.

"Oh well," continued the ass, "in that case what difference does it make to me whom I serve?"

To the poor, a change of government means no more than a change in the name of their master.

75 THE ARCHER AND THE LION

A skilful archer went to the mountains to hunt. As he approached, all the beasts fled - all, that is, except the lion who decided to challenge him. From quite a distance, the archer shot an arrow and wounded the lion:

"My arrow is my messenger," called the archer. "From it, you can gauge what I will be like when I attack you in person."

The lion fled in great fear and pain. A fox tried to restore his courage and chided him for running away after only the first attack.

"Save your breath," said the lion. "Anyone who sends such a devastating messenger must be very powerful indeed!"

It's very unpleasant to have a neighbour who can strike from a distance.

76 THE ASS AND THE FROGS

An ass carrying a heavy load of wood had to wade through a pond. As he was making his way, he tripped and fell over in the shallow water. Due to his heavy load, he was unable to get up and moaned and complained loudly. Some frogs in the water heard the ass and chided him:

"You're making such a silly fuss about a little tumble into the water. What on earth would you do if you had to live in this pond?"

Little grievances are borne with less courage than great misfortunes.

77   THE LION, THE ASS, AND THE FOX

The lion, the ass and the fox made a pact to assist each other in hunting. On their return with a large carcass, the lion asked the ass to divide the meat and give each member what they were due. The ass carefully made three equal portions out of the meat. On seeing this, the lion flew into a rage and ate the ass. After that, the lion asked the fox to divide the meat.

The fox carefully piled up most of the meat in front of the lion, keeping only a small scrap for himself. The lion was most pleased:

"My good fellow," he said to the fox, "from whom did you learn to divide like that?" To this, the fox replied humbly:

"I learnt it from the ass - just as you were devouring him."

Happy are they who learn from the misfortunes of others.

78 THE LAMP

An oil lamp filled with too much oil was burning vigorously and boasting that it was now brighter than the sun. A sudden squall blew it out. As the owner relit it, she muttered:

"Stop this showing-off and shine silently. Just remember, although dim, the stars never need to be relit."

Pride dazzles us and stops us from seeing our weaknesses.

79 THE LABOURER AND THE SNAKE

A snake, which had made its home under the porch of a labourer's cottage, bit the man's infant son, killing him with its venom. The next day the grief-stricken father decided to kill the snake. He waited outside the snake's hole. When the snake appeared, he rushed at it with his axe. In his haste, he missed the snake's head and only managed to cut off the end of its tail. Afraid that he might become the snake's next victim, the man attempted to make peace with the snake by placing a gift of bread and salt outside its hole. However, when the snake emerged it said to the man:

"There can never be peace between us, for whenever I see you, I remember losing my tail; and whenever you see me, you remember the son I took from you."

Injuries cannot be forgotten in the presence of the perpetrator.

80   THE BOY AND THE HAZELNUTS

A small boy put his hand into a jar full of hazelnuts. He grabbed as many hazelnuts as his hand could hold, only to find that he could not get his hand out of the narrow mouth of the jar. Not wanting to give up his hazelnuts, and unable to get his hand out, the little boy cried and complained bitterly. A wise friend came to his aid:

"Take half the number of hazelnuts, and your hand will come out easily."

Attempting too much at once is foolish.

81   THE MISER

A miser sold everything he owned and bought a large lump of gold, thinking that this was the best way to keep his wealth safe. He took the lump of gold and buried it in a hole in the ground and went to check it every day. One of the miser's workmen noticed his obsession with the place and guessed that treasure must be hidden there. Secretly, he dug it up and stole it. On his next visit, the miser was horrified to find the ground dug up and his lump of gold gone. Much grieved, he tore his hair and wept loudly. A neighbour, on learning of his misfortune, said:

"Don't upset yourself. Just get a stone, place it in the hole, and imagine you still have your gold. The stone will be just as useful to you, for when you had your gold you didn't do a thing with it!"

The true value of money resides in its use,
not simply in its accumulation.

82   THE HORSE AND THE GROOM

A groom would spend whole days brushing and rubbing down a horse. However, while giving the horse the best care, he stole his oats to supplement his income. One day, the horse said to the groom:

"If you truly wanted me to be in good condition, you would give me less grooming and more oats."

There is no better policy than honesty.

83   THE OXEN AND THE BUTCHERS

Once upon a time, the oxen decided that they would kill the butchers whose trade cost them their lives. On an appointed day, they all assembled and sharpened their horns in readiness to attack the butchers. They were about to make their attack, when an old ox, a veteran of many ploughed fields, spoke to the herd:

"They do indeed slaughter us," he said firmly, "however, they are highly skilled and cause no unnecessary pain. If we get rid of the butchers, we will be hacked to death by amateurs, and suffer a fate far worse than just death. Of this I am quite sure," he continued, "for the people will always demand beef."

Do not rush to exchange one evil for another.

84 THE FOX AND THE CROW

A crow stole a large piece of cheese and flew up into a high tree to enjoy it. A passing fox saw the cheese and decided to try and take it from her.

"The crow is such a fine bird," he exclaimed. "She is uniquely beautiful in both shape and complexion! It is a shame, though," he continued, "that her voice does not merit quite such praise. If it did, she would undoubtedly be regarded as the queen of all birds!"

The crow failed to detect the deceit in the fox's voice and thought she would show him just how beautifully she could sing. She gave a loud caw - her absolute best - and dropped the cheese. The fox quickly seized the cheese, and said to the crow:

"You certainly do have a voice, but where did you leave your brain?"

Flattery comes at a price.

85 THE OLD WOMAN AND THE WINE JAR

An old woman came across an empty jar that had contained exceptionally fine wine. She sniffed the jar cautiously and found that it retained a fruity fragrance. Closing her eyes, she drew in several breaths.

"How wonderful!" she exclaimed. "It must have been a delicious, superior wine to leave such a delightful aroma in the jar."

Good deeds live long in the memory.

86   THE TWO DOGS

A man trained one of his dogs to hunt and the other to guard his house. After hunting he would come home and give the guard dog a generous feed from the game bagged that day. The gun dog, who had worked hard, was put out by this:

"It's extremely unfair on me," he complained, "I have all the work while you just sit at home waiting for me to come back with your dinner!" The guard dog replied curtly:

"Don't blame me! It's not my fault our master hasn't taught me how to hunt. I never asked to become dependent on your labour."

It is wrong to blame children for the faults of their parents.

87   THE WILD BOAR AND THE FOX

A fox came across a wild boar sharpening his tusks against the trunk of a tree.

"Why do you spend so much time sharpening your tusks when neither hunter nor hound are anywhere to be seen?" inquired the fox.

"It is a precautionary measure," replied the wild boar emphatically, "there's no time to sharpen them once the hounds are tearing at me."

Preparedness guarantees readiness in an emergency.

88 THE ASS CARRYING A HOLY STATUE

A holy statue was being carried by an ass through the streets on its way to a temple. Passing through a crowd, many people bowed to the statue. The ass, thinking that they were honouring him, held his head up proudly and refused to move on. The driver whipped the ass fiercely and shouted:

"Oh, you foolish beast! We're not yet that degenerate as to pay homage to an ass."

The wise do not take credit due to others.

89   THE HUSBAND AND THE RUDE WIFE

A husband became displeased because his wife was always rude to their servants. To be sure that their servants weren't to blame, he found an excuse to send her to stay at his father's house. On her return, he inquired how she had got on with his father's staff.

"The cowhand and the shepherd frowned at me," she said bitterly.

"Well, that says it all!" replied the husband crossly. "Even the staff who were away from sunrise to sunset despised you. I hate to think how the staff who spent every day with you felt."

The bigger picture is revealed through small details.

90 THE PLOUGHMAN AND THE TREE

An old tree stood in the middle of a field. It bore no fruit but provided a roost for sparrows and cicadas. One day, the ploughman decided that it served no purpose and that the field would be better without it. However, when he struck the first blow with his axe, the sparrows and cicadas begged him to let them keep the tree as it provided a safe home for them. The ploughman ignored their pleas and continued to chop at the trunk.

Suddenly, bees flew out of the trunk, and there in the hollow tree were combs laden with honey. From then on the ploughman took good care of the old tree and regularly harvested the honey.

By nature, we are more driven by gain than justice.

91   THE FIR TREE AND THE BRAMBLE

A fir tree boasted to his neighbour, the bramble:

"You are of no use to anyone, while I am used in the construction of ships!" The bramble replied calmly:

"I think you have put the axes and saws, which cut you up, out of your mind. When you remember them, I'm sure you too would rather be a humble bramble."

A humble life without worries is preferable to a rich one with worries.

92   THE MAN BITTEN BY A DOG

A man who had received a nasty bite from a dog went in search of someone to heal him. On his way, he met a friend.

"Oh, that's easy enough," said the friend, "just take a piece of bread, soak it in blood from the wound and throw it to the dog who bit you." The man with the wound laughed at this advice and replied:

"If I did that, it would be like inviting every dog in the neighbourhood to bite me!"

Rewarding the evil only makes them stronger and more able to harm you.

93   THE MAN AND HIS DOG

A man prepared a wonderful dinner for an old family friend. However, his dog decided to invite a guest as well. The dog's guest arrived first and looked at all the delicacies beautifully laid out.

"This is sumptuous," he said, wagging his tail trustingly. "I'm going to eat so much; I won't need any food at all tomorrow!" Just then the cook came in, grabbed the dog by the hind legs and threw him out of the window. Howling, the dog made his way home. On the way, he came across some other dogs.

"Bet you had a good dinner," said one of them.

"Well, yes," replied the injured dog, "I drank so much that I don't even remember how I left the house."

Never trust those who are generous with the property of others.

94 THE HUNTSMAN AND THE FISHERMAN

On his return from a successful day's hunting, a huntsman met a fisherman who had made a good catch that day. The huntsman eyed the fish longingly and noticed the fisherman's interest in his game. They struck a happy bargain by exchanging the produce of the day's work. They were both so pleased with this arrangement that they continued to swap daily. One day a neighbour said to them:

'If you go on like this, you'll soon spoil the pleasure of your swap through familiarity, and you'll both want to keep your own produce."

Familiarity breeds contempt.

95   THE THIEF AND HIS MOTHER

A boy stole a schoolbook from one of his classmates. When he showed it to his mother she did not beat him but encouraged him to steal more. After this, he stole a cloak, for which she praised him even more. When the youth grew to be a man, he stole things of ever-greater value, until he was eventually caught red-handed.

With his hands bound behind him, he was led to the place of public execution. On seeing his distraught mother in the crowd, the young man asked to be allowed to say something into her ear. When she came close, he suddenly took her ear between his teeth and tore it off. The mother, in great agony, lamented the unnatural nature of her son. In response, the young man replied:

"If you had beaten me when I first stole the schoolbook, it would never have ended like this; and now I will suffer a disgraceful death."

A parent's failings become clearer over time.

96   THE OLD MAN AND DEATH

An old woodcutter had an extremely hard life. Every day he would cut wood in the forest and carry it to the city to sell. One day he was very tired. Exhausted, he let his load slip to the ground, lay down, and called to Death to come and take him. Death came straight away and asked why he had been called.

"Oh," stammered the old man, "I…err…I just thought you might be so kind and help me lift this load onto my shoulders."

The will to live is stronger than at first it might appear.

97   THE FOX AND THE MONKEY

The fox and the monkey were travelling together. As they walked along they argued about the nobility of their descent. Each listed his ancestors' distinctions and titles. As they passed a graveyard, the monkey stopped and sighed:

"It is hard not to shed tears when I think of all my noble ancestors buried here," he said. The fox looked at the monkey with a doubtful frown and said:

"You have very expertly picked a subject about which to lie; neither those buried here nor your ancestors will contradict you!"

A lie will often expose itself.

98 THE HART AND THE VINE

A hart fleeing from a hunter hid beneath the leaves of a large vine. The hunter passed the hart and went on his way. The hart, thinking that he was out of danger, started to nibble the leaves of the vine. When the hunter heard the rustle of leaves he came back and shot the hart with an arrow. As he was about to die, the hart said:

"I've brought this on myself; I should not have mistreated the vine that saved me."

Exploiting a benefactor is to tempt fate.

99   THE ASTRONOMER

Every night an astronomer went out to study the stars. One night as he was walking along, his entire attention focused on the sky, he stumbled and fell down a well. Scratched and bruised, he called loudly for help. A neighbour came to the well and, after hearing what had happened, said:

"You funny old fellow. You're so busy studying remarkable things in the sky that you fail to see what's here, right in front of your nose."

Lack of integrity in everyday life brings scorn on the heads of intellectuals.

100 THE CRAB AND HIS MOTHER

A mother crab reprimanded her son for walking sideways:

"It is so much more dignified to face the way you're going," she said. To this, the son replied indignantly:

"If you want to teach me, fine. Go ahead, I'll follow in your footsteps."

Practice what you preach.

101 THE FOX AND THE STORK

A fox, having invited a stork to supper, served soup in a flat dish. Every time the stork tried to drink, he only got the end of his long bill wet. The fox greatly enjoyed the stork's frustration.

"I do hope you will let me repay the compliment," said the stork calmly, as though nothing was wrong. "Tomorrow I'll provide the supper."

When the fox arrived to dine with the stork, he found he could not get at the food. He could only lick the drips from around the mouth of the exceptionally long, narrow-necked vessel in which the food had been served. Pretending to be unaware of the fox's distress, the long-billed stork ate heartily with the greatest of ease.

The hungry fox left with as much dignity as he could muster. He realised that he could not fault the stork for the hospitality skills he had taught him.

If you use cunning to mistreat others, expect to get paid back.

102 THE FOX AND THE MONKEY KING

A monkey so impressed an assembly of beasts that they elected him to be their king. A fox, who was very jealous of the monkey's crown and position, reported that he had discovered some meat, arguing that by rights it must surely be the property of the king.

When the monkey went to collect the meat, he was caught in a trap. The monkey immediately accused the fox of treachery. To this, the fox replied:

"I won't deny it, but did you honestly think that someone with a brain like yours could be king of all the animals?"

Ensure your choices are made for the right reasons.

103   THE CROW AND THE PITCHER

A crow, who was dying of thirst, found an abandoned pitcher. When he peered inside, he was very relieved to find that it contained some water. However, when he tried to drink, he found that he could not reach the water with his beak. The neck was too narrow and there was only a little water in the bottom of the pitcher. The crow tried everything he could think of but failed to get at the water.

Just as he was about to give up, he had an idea. He collected many pebbles and dropped them, one by one, into the pitcher. When the water had risen sufficiently he took a long drink and saved his life.

Necessity is the mother of invention.

104   THE MISCHIEVOUS DOG

A man tied a bell to his dog's collar to warn people that his dog often bites. The stupid dog became proud of his bell and was often seen in the marketplace showing off to other dogs. One day an old hound said to him:

"Must you make such a show of yourself? You behave as though the bell was given to you in recognition of some great deed. You would do well to remember that it marks you out as a menace to the public."

Notoriety should not be confused with fame.

105 THE SHEPHERD BOY AND THE WOLF

Close to a village, a shepherd boy tended his flock. When he became bored he would shout:

"Wolf! Wolf!"

When the villagers rushed to help him, he would simply laugh at them. He managed to insult them in this way on several occasions.

Then, one day, a wolf did come. The shepherd boy shouted with all his might, but no villagers came to help him. The wolf destroyed the entire flock at his leisure.

Even when liars speak the truth they are not believed.

106 THE BALD MAN AND THE FLY

A bald man slapped his head vigorously in an attempt to kill a fly that had bitten him. The fly escaped and taunted the man:

"You wished to kill me for a tiny bite. What will you do to yourself to revenge that hard slap?"

"That's not a problem," replied the bald man, "in this case, I know there was no intention to hurt me. I can't say the same for you, and I would happily have paid a higher price to see you destroyed."

Intentional harm hurts even more.

107 THE WIDOW AND THE SHEEP

A poor widow owned one sheep. When the time came to shear the sheep, she thought she would save money by shearing it herself. She was very clumsy; along with the wool, she cut off much flesh. In agony, the sheep said:

"Why are you hurting me like this? My flesh won't add to the value of the wool; you should hire a shearer. Or, if you want to sell me for mutton, pay the butcher to kill me quickly."

> *There is more to economics than the avoidance of expenses.*

108   THE ASS AND THE CHARGER

An ass admired and envied the lifestyle of a well-fed horse and lamented his own hard life and lack of food. However, when war broke out a man mounted the horse and rode into the thick of battle. The horse was injured and died on the battlefield.

When the ass heard the news he changed his mind and felt nothing but pity for the horse.

A life can only be judged in its entirety.

109   THE BEE AND JUPITER

A bee flew up to Mount Olympus to present Jupiter with an offering of honey from her combs. Jupiter was most pleased with the gift and promised to grant her any wish she might have.

"Oh," said the bee, much delighted, "please give me a sting so that I can attack any man who tries to take my honey."

Jupiter was not happy with this request, for he was very fond of humans. He could not refuse, though, as he had promised to give the bee anything she might wish for. He thought hard and said:

"Very well, you shall have a sting in your tail, but there is a price for using it. If you sting someone, the sting will remain in the wound, and you will die from its loss."

Like chickens, evil wishes come home to roost.

110 THE OAK AND THE REEDS

A violent storm uprooted a large oak tree and threw it down among the reeds. Dejected, the old oak asked the reeds:

"How do you survive unbroken? You look so thin and weak." The reeds replied:

"You, so strong and rigid, fight the wind and are eventually beaten. We, who are very flexible, bend before the wind and let him pass."

Win by knowing when not to fight.

111 THE KID AND THE WOLF

A kid climbed up onto the roof of a house. When a wolf came by, the kid taunted him from her position of safety. The wolf stopped and said:

"Little goat, I hear what you are saying. However, it is not you that is mocking me, it is the roof that is protecting you."

Time and place can give temporary strength to the weak.

112 THE DOG AND THE HARE

A dog startled a hare and chased it across the hillside. Sometimes he would catch up with the hare and bite it, and at other times he would fawn upon the hare as though he was just playing with another dog. Infuriated, the hare said to the dog:

"I wish you would make up your mind! If you are my friend, then don't bite me; if you are my enemy, then don't fawn over me."

Without trust, there can be no real friendship.

113   THE DOG AND THE OYSTER

A dog accustomed to a diet of eggs found an oyster. Supposing it to be an egg, he swallowed it down in one go. Not long afterwards, the dog suffered severe stomach cramps and reprimanded himself bitterly:

"I deserve this, I know. How stupid I was to assume that all round-looking things are eggs!"

Think before you act.

114 THE HORSE AND THE STAG

A horse, who had a meadow all to himself, was most offended when a stag ate his grass. Unable to take revenge on his own, he approached a man for help. The man thought about it carefully and said:

"I will help you, but you must let me put a bit in your mouth and let me ride you." The horse agreed to this and has been serving us ever since.

The cost of revenge may be high.

115 THE SICK STAG

A sick stag lay down in the corner of the pasture where there was plenty of grass for him within easy reach. Many of his friends came to ask after his health. As much as he enjoyed the visits, each visitor ate the grass from around him. In the end, the stag died of starvation and not from his illness.

Thoughtless friends can do great harm.

116 THE FROGS ASKING FOR A KING

The frogs sent an ambassador to Jupiter to ask for a king. Realising just how simple they were, Jupiter gave them a large log, which he hurled into their lake with a great splash. Initially, they were terrified of their new king and hid themselves. However, after a while, they realised that their king was harmless. It was not long before they showed their contempt for the log by squatting on it.

On becoming dissatisfied with their inert ruler, they again asked Jupiter for a king. This time he gave them an eel. But once again, they were dissatisfied with their kindly ruler.

When they asked Jupiter for the third time to give them a king, he got cross and sent them a heron. Every day, the heron ate frogs until there were no frogs left. Unsurprisingly, no further requests were made to Jupiter.

Do not rush to make changes, unless you are sure it is for the better.

117 THE FISHERMAN AND THE LITTLE FISH

After a long, hard day's work, a fisherman found just one little fish in his nets.

"Put me back," pleaded the little fish. "I wouldn't be more than a mouthful for you. Besides, when I'm fully grown you can catch me again."

"What do you take me for?" said the fisherman, shaking his head. "I've got you now; in the future, you'll try to avoid my nets, as always."

Only fools gamble an actual gain for a highly unlikely greater profit.

118 THE VAIN CROW

A vain crow planned to join a flock of peacocks by sticking some feathers they had shed among his own feathers.

"Bye-bye, it's been good knowing you," he said to his old friends, looking down his beak, and strutted off. When he reached the flock of peacocks, he introduced himself with great confidence. However, the peacocks were not fooled. Angrily, they snatched back their feathers, pecking him violently with their beaks. Injured and scruffy, he limped back to his own flock of crows.

"So," they crowed raucously, "suddenly we're good enough for you again? It's not what kind of feathers you have that matters but how you treat others."

And so, the vain crow was driven from the flock.

Snubbed friends are slow to forgive.

119   THE HARE AND THE HOUND

An exhausted hound lay on the ground panting heavily, having failed to catch a hare. A passing goatherd, having watched the chase, mocked him:

"The little hare beat you! He got away!"

"I see you haven't thought about this very much," replied the hound. "There's a world of difference between running for your supper and running for your life."

Never underestimate the importance of motivation.

120 THE DOLPHINS, THE WHALES, AND THE SPRAT

At the height of a war between the dolphins and the whales, a sprat offered to mediate. In reply, one of the dolphins called out scornfully:

"We would all rather perish than have *you* trying to reconcile our differences!"

Mediators must command the respect of all parties.

121 THE BOY AND THE NETTLE

A boy who had been stung by a nettle said to his mother:
 "I only touched it gently, and then it stung me."
 "That's exactly the reason it stung you," replied the boy's mother. "Next time you handle a nettle grasp it firmly, and it will not sting you."

If you have decided to do something, do it with conviction.
Grasp the nettle!

122 THE FOX AND THE LION

When a fox saw a lion for the first time, he was so frightened he thought he would die. When he met the lion for the second time, he was still afraid but managed not to let it show. On meeting the lion for the third time, the fox felt confident enough to go up to him and have a chat.

Familiarity breeds contempt.

123 THE MULE

Feeling frisky from eating too much corn, a mule was galloping, and jumping around in his field, when a wonderful thought occurred to him:

"My mother must have been a great racehorse – and I'm just as fast!"

Later, though, when he had worn himself out, he suddenly remembered that his father had been an ass.

There are at least two sides to the truth.

124 THE HAWK, THE KITE, AND THE PIGEONS

The pigeons lived in constant fear of attack from a kite. When a hawk offered them protection in exchange for becoming their king, they readily agreed. However, once the hawk had settled into the dovecot, he ate pigeons every day. In fact, he ate more pigeons in a week than the kite would have taken in a year.

Some cures are worse than the disease.

125 THE MILLER, HIS SON, AND THEIR ASS

A miller and his son were on their way to market to sell an ass. As they passed a group of women at a well, they overheard one woman saying:

"Just look at that! Two fellows walking and no one riding!"

The old man quickly lifted his son onto the ass and continued to walk alongside. They had not gone far when they passed a group of old men.

"You see what I mean," said one of them loudly, "old people just don't get the respect they deserve, these days. Shame on the boy! He should let his old father rest his aching limbs." On hearing this, the father made the boy dismount and seated himself on the ass. Presently, they met a group of women and children:

"Poor little boy," cried several voices at once, "he can hardly keep up with his lazy father!" The patient miller lifted his son, and they rode on together.

"Is that your ass?" a man asked indignantly, just as they were approaching the town.

"Yes," replied the miller.

"I wouldn't have guessed by the way you overload him!" replied the man. "You two look like you could carry him better than he can carry you."

"We'll give it a go," said the miller. And so, they tied the ass's feet to a stout pole. The miller shouldered one end, the boy the other. By the time they reached the bridge that led over the river and into the town, a large jeering crowd surrounded them. The ass, already distressed from being hung upside down, struggled violently, broke the ropes, and fell into the river.

Angry and humiliated, the miller and his son made their way home on foot. In the end, the miller had not been able to please anyone and had lost his ass.

If you try to please everyone, you end up pleasing no one.

INDEX OF FABLE TITLES

N.B. Numbers refer to the fable number in this book – they are not page numbers.

Ants and Grasshopper	11
Archer and Lion	75
Ass and Charger	108
Ass and Frogs	76
Ass and his Purchaser	55
Ass and Old Shepherd	74
Ass and Wolf	46
Ass Carrying Holy Statue	88
Ass, Fox, and Lion	28
Astronomer	99
Bald Man and Fly	106
Bat and Weasels	5
Bear and Fox	27

INDEX OF FABLE TITLES

Bear and Two Travellers	35
Bee and Jupiter	109
Boasting Traveller	10
Boy and Hazelnuts	80
Boy and Nettle	121
Boy Bathing	44
Boy Hunting Locusts	9
Charcoal Burner and Fuller	8
Cock and Jewel	12
Crab and his Mother	100
Crow and Pitcher	103
Crow and Sheep	65
Dog and Hare	112
Dog and his Reflection	18
Dog and Oyster	113
Dog in Manger	36
Dogs and Hides	42
Dolphins, Whales, and Sprat	120
Donkey and Grasshoppers	6
Dove and Crow	54
Eagle and Crow	56
Farmer and Cranes	33
Farmer and Fox	53
Farmer and Snake	21
Farmer and Stork	23

INDEX OF FABLE TITLES

Father and his Sons	3
Fawn and his Mother	24
Fir Tree and Bramble	91
Fisherman and Little Fish	117
Fisherman Piping	14
Flea and Man	59
Flies and Honey Pot	29
Fox and Crow	84
Fox and Goat	32
Fox and Grapes	67
Fox and Leopard	50
Fox and Lion	122
Fox and Monkey	97
Fox and Monkey King	102
Fox and Stork	101
Frogs Asking for a King	116
Hare and Hound	119
Hare and Tortoise	15
Hares and Foxes	71
Hares and Frogs	40
Hares and Lions	45
Hart and Vine	98
Hawk, Kite, and Pigeons	124
Hercules and Wagoner	17
Herdsman and Lost Calf	22

INDEX OF FABLE TITLES

Horse and Groom	82
Horse and Stag	114
Huntsman and Fisherman	94
Husband and Rude Wife	89
Kid and Wolf	111
Kingdom of the Lion	13
Kites and Swans	73
Labourer and Snake	79
Lamb and Wolf	63
Lamp	78
Lion and Eagle	58
Lion and Mouse	1
Lion, Ass, and Fox	77
Lion in Love	20
Lioness	34
Man and his Dog	93
Man and Lion	30
Man Bitten by Dog	92
Miller, his Son, and their Ass	125
Mischievous Dog	104
Miser	81
Mole and his Mother	19
Mountain in Labour	26
Mule	123
Mules and Robbers	61

INDEX OF FABLE TITLES

North Wind and Sun	48
Oak and Reeds	110
Old Man and Death	96
Old Woman and Wine Jar	85
Oxen and Axles	38
Oxen and Butchers	83
Partridge and Fowler	64
Philosopher, Ants, and Mercury	52
Ploughman and Tree	90
Pomegranate, Apple Tree, and Bramble	25
Prophet	68
Quack Frog	47
Rich Man and Tanner	62
Shepherd Boy and Wolf	105
Sick Lion	2
Sick Stag	115
Sparrow and Hare	66
Stag at Pool	41
Thief and his Mother	95
Thieves and Cock	49
Thirsty Pigeon	37
Tortoise and Eagle	31
Traveller and Fortune	51
Traveller and his Dog	16
Trumpeter Taken Prisoner	43

INDEX OF FABLE TITLES

Two Bags	57
Two Dogs	86
Two Frogs	70
Vain Crow	118
Viper and File	60
Widow and Sheep	107
Wild Boar and Fox	87
Wolf and Crane	7
Wolf and Fox	69
Wolf and Lamb	4
Wolf in Sheep's Clothing	39
Woman and her Hen	72

READER'S PERSONAL NOTES

PERSONAL NOTES

PERSONAL NOTES

PERSONAL NOTES

PERSONAL NOTES

PERSONAL NOTES

PERSONAL NOTES

PERSONAL NOTES

PERSONAL NOTES

PERSONAL NOTES

PERSONAL NOTES

PERSONAL NOTES